The Zombie Inside

THE ZOMBIE INSIDE

Moon Laramie

This edition first published in 2016 by
Martin Firrell Company Limited
26 Red Lion Square, London, WC1R 4AG.
Cover painting by Langham Bailey.
www.moonlaramie.com

ISBN 978-0-9931786-2-7

The Zombie Inside is intended as a general
guide to focusing thoughts positively.
It is not a substitute for any professional
medical or psychiatric advice or treatment.
Any actions you may take as a result of reading
The Zombie Inside are your own responsibility
and taken at your own risk. The author and
publisher can assume no responsibility for
any individual's actions or any effect caused
by them.

Most of the time we ignore our own amazing potential, settling instead for a life of 'limitation and lack' – personified rather brilliantly by Moon Laramie as our 'inner zombie'. Our zombie, he says, sabotages us whenever we put our heads above the parapet and dare to dream.

The Zombie Inside is full of helpful tips and strategies for attracting the life we long for. It is simply and clearly written and illustrated with very human anecdotes from Moon's own struggle with his inner zombie. And it's a salutary reminder that we really do have a choice about how we live.

Being a modern guru, Moon co-opts the smart phone as our ally. He suggests we load inspirational words, uplifting music, affirmations and positive comments about ourselves and others, make FaceTime with our 'abundance buddy', and then access them throughout the day, whenever we feel the pull of our inner zombie dragging us back down. Good plan, considering, as Moon says, most of us are wedded to our phones 24/7.

We must learn to act and think as if we are already confident adventurers exploring life's riches. By this trick of what Moon calls 'positive knowing', we can gradually change the DNA of our lives.

HILARY BOYD
hilaryboyd.com

THANKS

The author would like to thank the following people for their help and inspiration:

Martin Firrell, Carly Lewisohn, Langham Bailey, Jason Heath, Hilary Boyd.

TABLE OF CONTENTS

PREFACE

PREFACE

In 2008 I believed I was washed up. I was forty-two. I was in a civil partnership that I was increasingly disillusioned with. I was following a career I hated and it had made me ill. I was overweight and sad. I felt I'd had my one chance at life and blown it. That was the way it was. That was my lot in life. Others had it better. Too bad.

At that time, I had just begun to discover the ideas of New Thought and something called the Law of Attraction. Intrigued by the results others had described, I began to apply these ideas to my own life. I wanted them to become second nature. I wanted to form a daily habit of thinking and acting in more productive ways.

Now I have a career I love, my perfect partner, my perfect body. I enjoy the company of people I admire. I have the resources to travel anywhere in the world. I get up when I please and spend my days in ways I find interesting and fulfilling.

This book shares the ideas I used to alter my thinking. I changed the quality of my inner dialogue from self-doubting to self-believing. As a result, my life changed from plain existence to a life rich with rewarding experiences. The same can be true for you.

PART ONE

THE UNIVERSAL LAW OF ATTRACTION

You've noticed there's something going on but you can't quite put your finger on it. It's that feeling you have on 'one of those days' when everything seems to go wrong. Or that feeling you have when things seem to fall effortlessly into place for you, one after the other. Your feelings can be so intuitive on these occasions that you can almost feel the good or the bad rushing towards you. This is hardly surprising because this is precisely what's happening to you. Although most people don't realise it, there is a powerful force at work in all our lives. It's the universal Law of Attraction and it is a natural law governed by our thoughts and actions. This law is enacted by Universal Mind, and it is through Universal Mind that we are all connected.

The Law of Attraction is a natural law like the law of gravity. It is working all the time for every one of us and it works on the principle that like attracts like. Universal Mind connects us to each other and to the material Universe that we collectively perceive.

Charles F. Haanel writes in his ground-breaking book, The Master Key System, 'The Universal Mind is static, or potential, energy. It simply is. It can manifest only through the individual, and the individual can manifest only through the Universal. They are one.'

Human beings, our thoughts and the Universe we inhabit are made up of energy. If like energy attracts like energy, then positive thoughts attract positive people and circumstances. We are each an individual thought magnet connected to the whole. We are each creating our own world through our thoughts, whether those thoughts are positive or negative. Therefore, if we focus on positive thoughts, we attract other people and events that are on that same positive frequency.

YOUR INNER ZOMBIE

But there is always something holding us back. It's that inner voice that expresses a lack of belief in ourselves and our abilities. It's the undermining self-talk that says, 'I don't really deserve the things I want. I'm not good enough.' This is a toxic lie. We need to re-train ourselves to stifle that voice inside. It is poisonous with doubt about the true potential of life. It says, 'Know your place. You had better be careful. Life is hard and full of knocks.'

This description of the world curtails life's potential. It is the product of a limited belief system. Unchecked, it will prevent us from living our lives to their fullest. This narrative exists inside most of us to a lesser or greater degree. It leads us to believe that our worth is limited. It suggests that there is nothing special about us when, in truth, everyone is unique. Everyone can have a remarkable life, no matter who they are or where they start from. It only requires small changes in the way we think. Learn to tap into the potential of the Law of Attraction. Learn to become aware of the voice inside and the statements it makes. Negative self-talk encourages us to settle for less than we really want. Negative self-talk is like one of the living dead, shuffling along, merely existing and suggesting we do the same. This is the voice of your inner zombie. Like any B-movie zombie, it can attack at any time. Its weapons of choice are doubt, fear and pathological pessimism. It will drag you into a quagmire of self-limiting belief. Once it gets a firm grip, it will haul you farther and farther into its shadow-realm. You must be on your guard. Sometimes it can be difficult to discern what is actually happening. You may be experiencing legitimate doubt that will help you make a more prudent decision. Or the doubt may be entirely spurious, the insidious and self-limiting murmurings of your inner zombie. It's imperative that we learn to tell the difference. It's equally imperative to learn how to take decisive action. It is no exaggeration to say that your life depends on it.

Most of us have been raised to believe our lives must be limited. We've been raised to believe we must exist within certain parameters of life-possibility. Your inner zombie is the ultimate mouthpiece for this train of thought. The truth is very different. Your life has no predetermined limits. You can be who you want to be. You can earn your income in the way you prefer. You can love and be loved. You can have a richly rewarding relationship with other people and the world at large.

YOUR INNER ADVENTURER

There is another voice inside you. It is the voice that says, 'I deserve the things I want. I am good enough. Life can be a wonderful adventure.' This voice speaks only of potential and possibility. This is the voice of your inner adventurer. It tells you a story of life as something limitless. It suggests your life can be infinitely rich and fulfilling. It expresses the firm belief that both plenty and happiness are your birthright. Your inner adventurer always maintains that great things will happen to you. You already have good things in your life, no matter how small. Your inner adventurer encourages you to be thankful and joyful for those things. Your adventurer speaks only about the best to attract the best. Your adventurer invariably expresses an unwaveringly positive view of the world. Positive thought attracts a positive outcome. Your adventurer advocates this as a fundamental truth, as an inevitability.

THE STRUGGLE BETWEEN YOUR INNER ZOMBIE AND YOUR INNER ADVENTURER

We are all natural-born adventurers. As children we dress up, we make believe, we imagine daring adventures and expect the world to be an expansive and exciting place to explore. But as we grow up we are taught to view our innate sense of adventure as increasingly unrealistic. We are told that having a life full of playfulness is a nice idea, a lovely little pipe dream, but in reality it doesn't work out like that. As we grow up we don't play or use our imaginations so much. It's implied that life is something that simply happens to us. We're told we must take what life throws at us and aim to get a good job so we don't starve. Education and adulthood place the ideas of fear, limitation and lack in the forefront of our minds. The focus is on caution, on what we can't do. We're taught to believe that life is full of toil and uncertainty over which we have little or no control. We grow up internalising feelings of lessened expectation and disappointment. This sets the scene for the rise of the inner zombie.

This lessening of possibility happens regardless of who we are, whatever race, culture, identity or any other variable. As we mature into adulthood our sense of adventure becomes dampened down. We become less expansive of spirit. Our inner zombie slowly takes control of our life story and we identify more and more closely with negative frequencies which must bring negative things into our lives. But if we can learn to pay closer attention to the voice of our inner adventurer as we mature, we can connect to positive frequencies which, by the same token, must bring the positive into our lives.

Ever since you were born, you have been fed ideas of limited expectation. The voice of your inner zombie has been amplified and endorsed by parents, guardians and teachers. This means your inner zombie has been made stronger than your inner adventurer. Each time you move in a positive direction, your inner zombie will resist. Are you content to let this happen? Or are you prepared to take action? Are you prepared to rebel against the status quo? Are you ready to concentrate your attention more fully on the voice of your inner adventurer? This book will help you augment the power of your inner adventurer and challenge your zombie's destructive narrative. It will enable you to change your thoughts and reflect those thoughts in your actions. You will learn how to use the power of your smart phone to steer your thoughts and actions positively. You will learn how to pay greater attention to the voice of your inner adventurer every day and drown out the voice of your inner zombie.

The voice of your inner zombie is not your authentic voice. It is an imposter. You are the only one with genuine power. It's time to take control. It's time to seize and exercise that power now.

CHOOSE YOUR THOUGHTS CONSCIOUSLY TO MOVE IN THE DIRECTION OF YOUR GOALS

The Law of Attraction is working all the time. We cannot switch it on or off. Negative will attract negative. Positive will attract positive. By consciously choosing to focus on positive thoughts and behaviours we can begin to take control. Belief precedes reality and expectation is the mould into which the jelly of reality flows. Our current lives are the results of our previous beliefs, thoughts and actions. If we want to improve our lives we need to improve the way we think. We need to turn a deaf ear to the voice of our inner zombie and start paying closer attention to the positive voice of our inner adventurer.

By taking the counsel of your inner adventurer you will feel better. You will begin to attract into your life more of the things you really value. Your life will have more of the qualities you wish for it and less of the qualities your inner zombie's narrative once described as inevitable.

Any aspect of life can be transformed. You can find your perfect partner. You can find the ideal way to earn your income. You can be anyone you want to be. You can live life on your own terms.

When you change your thoughts, change in your life is inevitable. But it may not be immediate. Most body builders will tell you that successful bodybuilding relies on concerted effort over time. Half of the increase in muscle growth comes from your diet. Half comes from the weights you are lifting. It is the same with manifesting change through the Law of Attraction. It's important to focus on the outcomes you want to see and expect to realise them. But that is only half of the task. The other half consists of moving consciously in the direction of your intended goals. Sitting at home fantasising about being a film star is not a realistic way of turning that desire into a reality.

Take the first step and join a drama group or sign up for acting classes. Focused intention is only one half of the story. Direct action is the other half. Working on both halves concurrently will generate the change you want to see.

This book will support you as you take action towards your goal. It will guide you to think, act and feel as if you already have what you want. Doing so mobilises the Law of Attraction in powerful and unexpected ways. Heighten your senses. Become more aware of your internal narrative. Practice listening for which voice is dominant at any one time. Is this the voice of your inner zombie or your inner adventurer? Becoming more aware of your mental state is the first step towards changing it.

FOCUS ON WHAT YOU WANT, NOT ON WHAT YOU DON'T WANT

It's part of the human experience to focus on things we fear will happen. When we focus on our fears, we amplify them and give them more energy. The more we think about what we don't want, the quicker it materialises. Here's an example that illustrates this quirk in human nature. A good friend of mine, who lived in the countryside in Dorset, was coming to stay with me in London. Being used to a less hurried way of life, she talked often about how unbearably fast London seemed to her. She would say how much she hated the London Underground because of the volume of people jostling against one another in a confined space.

There is some truth in what my friend was saying, of course. London is one of the fastest moving cities in the world and the London Underground moves millions of people each week. I was a regular user of the underground and had developed a strategy for coping with the crowds. My inner zombie would tell me to prepare for the worst. Instead, I chose to pay attention to the voice of my inner adventurer. Whenever I was on a crowded train, I would find a point of calm within. I would listen to relaxing music or an audio book on the Law of Attraction. This would have the effect of immersing me in a peaceful soundscape and distancing me from the feeling of being jostled or hemmed in. Emotionally, it was as if I had taken myself out of the situation entirely.

My subjective experience of the underground was determined by my adventurer's insistence on finding inner tranquility in a challenging situation. As a consequence, my experience was radically different from that of my friend. She would find herself in train carriages with standing room only and then the train would be delayed, stuck in a tunnel. This happened to me much more rarely even though I travelled on the underground more often. I expected the best from the London Underground. I did not expect to be jostled. I did not expect to be delayed. I manifested a positive experience through the Law of Attraction. My friend manifested a negative experience through the action of the same law.

On the day my friend came to stay with me, she spent a long time telling me how much she hated the underground. Her inner zombie had taken control of her narrative. She went into the experience expecting the worst. She was agitated and tense as we boarded the train. What happened to her next reflected the power of the Law of Attraction. People knocked into her. People brushed against her as they got on and off the train. One man backed into her and someone else swung round with a large bag knocking her legs out from under her. As each of these events happened, she became increasingly irritated, so attracting more experiences of the same kind to her. All of this took place in a half empty carriage. By contrast, my personal space remained undisturbed. The next day, the pattern was repeated. The forces at work were the same. My friend experienced similar invasions into her personal space. I experienced no disturbance at all even though I was beside her throughout the journey.

If you believe something is true and put your energy and emotion into that belief then it will become true for you. To what degree do you want your truth to be negative or positive? To what degree are you prepared to let your inner zombie dominate your narrative? Are you prepared to be dragged down into the zomboid slime? Or do you have the resolve to wrest the narrative away from the negative? Giving your inner adventurer control will set you on course for the more carefree and upbeat experiences you deserve.

THE POWER OF PLAYFULNESS

When you feel playful, you are much closer to your inner adventurer than your inner zombie. Playfulness and adventure are intimately related. The word 'adventure' conveys the idea of a playful or enjoyable experience. An adventure film is a spirited story full of exciting incident. An adventure ride at a theme park is an electrifying journey full of thrills and spills. Excitement, adventure, and play are all powerfully linked. Being playful changes the energy around you. When you feel playful, you feel lighter inside. People respond to you in a more lighthearted and good-natured way. The

Laughing Buddha is a beloved figure in Chinese folklore. Though poor, he laughs at life. He is able to laugh because he is content. Children love him and follow him because of the playful energy he radiates. Laughing makes him a magnet for good fortune. He is so loved because he is lucky, laughing and lighthearted. He is animated by his lightness of spirit.

Your inner zombie feeds on solemnity and the idea that life is a serious and grave thing. A playful atmosphere is noxious for it. Playfulness stifles your inner zombie and robs it of energy. Its power to influence you diminishes.

Adults are so often discouraged from playing. It's implied that seriousness makes a legitimate and credible grown-up. Adults have jobs to do, goals to achieve, responsibilities to meet. There is no time for frivolity. But playfulness is a critical skill. It is through the action of playfulness that your inner zombie is most easily silenced. The quality of your future depends on your ability to be playful. We need to reclaim our right to play. We need to re-skill ourselves in this forgotten art. It is as if we have a muscle that is wasted. We need to build it up and make it strong again. Learn to have serious fun like China's Laughing Buddha. Through serious fun you connect directly with the playful nature of your inner adventurer.

THE POWER OF POSITIVE KNOWING

I was talking to a small group of people about my work with the Law of Attraction. I was describing the struggle between the inner zombie and the inner adventurer. One of the people in the group turned to me and said, 'It's positive thinking isn't it?' When I thought about this later, I felt more and more that this view was misleading. It was a crude simplification.

What we are talking about is not positive thinking. Positive thinking suggests putting on a brave face. Positive thinking suggests soldiering on in spite of adversity. What we are talking about instead is positive knowing. There is a big difference between the two. Positive knowing is a firm and unyielding expectation that underpins positive action and brings about lasting change for the good.

In positive knowing you are absolutely sure of the outcome, no matter what evidence appears to the contrary. Positive knowing has a determined but relaxed quality to it.

After my divorce, I moved back to London. I was living at my father's house. I knew almost nobody and was saving for a mortgage. These conditions made me extremely susceptible to the murmurings of my inner zombie. I was washed up. I was too old to be considered attractive. I would struggle to find a decent property to buy. I would have to make do with a home I didn't really like. At least it would be a roof over my head. This was complete nonsense of course, but our inner zombie will always rise up most powerfully when times are tough. I decided to make a deliberate effort to quieten the voice of my inner zombie by focusing on what I really wanted. I made the conscious decision to listen instead to the affirmative voice of my inner adventurer.

I had started a new job at the children's charity UNICEF UK. I was meeting committed people and talking about an inspiring project. There was energy in this new phase of my career and I focused on this energy to create a positive mental foothold. I began the search for an apartment. First of all I thought about the features that were really important to me. I created an exact picture of my requirements in my mind's eye. I then wrote down those requirements clearly and put the piece of paper on the wall opposite my bed.

Two-bedroom apartment, leafy area of London, top floor, secure entry system, pleasant neighbours, fair price, freehold.

Property prices had slumped in London so I was in an advantageous financial position. However, media commentary suggested that a new property boom was on the horizon. Prices would soon rise again sharply. Rather than panic, I reflected on the nature of news reporting itself. A bad news story is always good for ratings. But this particular bad news story was not good for me so I gave it neither my energy nor my attention. Estate agents told me that it would be impossible to get a freehold apartment. I decided to remain undeterred and to take my time. I decided to be the assured adventurer confident I would get exactly what I wanted. After viewing one particularly disappointing property, my sister remarked on the apartment buildings opposite. Avondale Court had beautiful ornamental gardens and pretty slate roofs.

'I've heard that the apartments there are supposed to be lovely inside,' she said.

When I asked the estate agent about the building, he told me there were no apartments for sale in Avondale Court and a home there would be at least £30,000 beyond my price range. Undeterred, I continued my search neither panicked nor in a rush.

Universal Mind has one particular quality that is of immense importance to your inner adventurer. Universal Mind cannot distinguish between what is real and what is pretended. If you act as if something is already true for you, the Law of Attraction will follow your lead and bring that truth into being. I decided to apply this principle to the task of finding my ideal home.

South Woodford was the area I wanted to live in. This neighbourhood had a village-like quality with leafy streets and pretty shops and cafes. It was on the edge of East London and fifteen miles from my father's house in Ongar, Essex. Mindful that the Law of Attraction cannot discern between the actual and the imagined, I decided to act as if I lived at Avondale Court already. Every day, I drove to South Woodford, parked outside Avondale Court and took the train from there into London for work. I did this religiously even if it was freezing cold or snowing. This added an extra half hour to my journey each day but I was determined to act the part of someone who already had a home in South Woodford. I believed wholeheartedly that acting 'as if' would activate the Law of Attraction to make my desire come true for me. One morning, as I was walking from the apartment building to the station, a voice in my head said, 'Take a look at that estate agent's window.' As I looked in the window, I thought to myself, 'There you are!' An apartment in Avondale Court had just come onto the market. My next thought was, 'It works.' The Universe had begun to manifest my desire. I felt certain that all I had to do was continue in the same vein. Be assured. Maintain the unwavering mind of a confident adventurer.

I viewed the apartment and loved it. I took a picture of the outside and saved it as the wallpaper on my smart phone. Every time I looked at my phone, I saw Avondale Court. We all look at our phones countless times a day. My phone became a powerful tool, helping me focus on the apartment over and over again. Full of confidence, I made an offer.

It was rejected.

I was disappointed but I was not fazed. I now had a pin-sharp focus for my daily commute. Each day I would park outside Avondale Court and walk to the station. I would listen to uplifting music, immersed in the role of Moon Laramie, the carefree owner of his ideal home in South Woodford.

I made further offers for the apartment and they too were rejected. So I stopped making offers. I continued my daily ritual regardless, positively knowing that the property would eventually be mine. I photocopied the estate agent's letterhead and retyped the agent's letters rejecting my offers. I changed the wording in each case from rejection to acceptance. I took a copy of the property details and wrote across the top 'thank you' in bold red ink. I addressed envelopes to myself as if I already lived at the apartment. I asked a friend who was also familiar with the Law of Attraction to send me an email congratulating me on my purchase. I placed all of these pieces of paper on the wall opposite my bed. They were the last things I saw at night and the first things I saw in the morning. They reinforced my resolve to act as if I owned the property already.

But then the voice of my inner zombie sounded loudly again in my head, 'You should give up. The apartment is beyond your price range. You're wasting your efforts. Someone else is bound to get it.' It was difficult to hear. At the same time, it was not unexpected. It's in the nature of the inner zombie to latch onto any setback and amplify it. I listened carefully to the tone of the voice in my head and heard it for what it was. It was zomboid nonsense. When you realise you are hearing the voice of your inner zombie, you can dismiss the content of the narrative. The inner zombie always makes the same case. It always talks about what is not possible or what will go wrong. These moanings are of no use to us. They are empty and meaningless. With practice, it's possible to exploit the voice of your inner zombie to heighten your resolve. You could say to yourself, 'I must be on the right track because the zombie inside is agitated and worried that I am about to succeed.' You can choose to regard your inner zombie's increasing prattle as a bellwether, indicating success is close by.

I chose to do just that and redouble my efforts. I allowed myself to be guided by my understanding of the difference between expecting and needing. When you expect something, you attract reasons to support your expectation. When you need something, you attract reasons to support your neediness. Listen to the words themselves. Expect, expectation, expectancy all have connotations of manifestation. Something is going to happen or appear. Need, needy, neediness all have connotations of lack. Something is going to be scarce or remain out of reach. If you find yourself thinking, 'I need,' change the narrative to, 'I expect.' The Law of Attraction responds to both equally. It brings reasons to need to the needy, and reasons to expect to the expectant. The inner zombie is always full of neediness. The inner adventurer is always full of expectation.

For many weeks I had been acting as if I already owned my ideal apartment. I had remained undeterred when my offers were rejected. I knew I was doing everything possible to activate the Law of Attraction. I did not feel needy. I felt confident of the outcome. I drove to the apartment building as usual, parked outside, and made my way to work. It was then that the estate agent called. She said there had been no other offers for the property and asked if I was still interested in buying. After a short negotiation, we agreed the price. I purchased the apartment for exactly the amount I intended. The vendors and the estate agent very kindly made a generous donation to UNICEF as well.

And the apartment was exactly as described in my original wish list: two bedrooms, top floor, secure entry system, freehold and with pleasant neighbours.

This outcome manifested because I had acted as if the apartment was already mine. I had expected rather then needed. I had successfully identified the skullduggery of my zombie and heard it for what it was which enabled me to disregard it. Like a self-assured adventurer, I expected to get what I wanted. And I did.

THE MIND-SET MANTRA

If you apply the principle of acting 'as if', you will begin to manifest your desires. The change you want may take time to appear or you may encounter setbacks on your journey. Then it can be challenging to remain motivated. Mind-set mantras can be a great help in staying true to your original intention.

Mind-set mantras are short phrases that neutralise deep-rooted, negative beliefs about yourself. These beliefs are often based on feelings of low self-worth and they sabotage your work with the Law of Attraction. Mind-set mantras begin with the words, 'I deserve,' 'It is right that,' 'I am worthy of,' 'It is just.'

By referring to your mantras frequently and repeating them to yourself, you begin to re-programme your subconscious belief system. Use the notes section on your smart phone to develop a list of mind-set mantras and look at them often.

Think about your future plans and say to yourself, 'It is right that I have these changes in my life.' If you are looking for your perfect partner, your mind-set mantra could be as simple as, 'I deserve my perfect partner.' If you are looking for a new career, say, 'I am worthy of this new career.'

The inner adventurer helps the Law of Attraction to do its job by expecting rather than needing. Like must attract like. Expectation brings that which is expected. It is inevitable.

Part One of The Zombie Inside has described the principle of the Law of Attraction. You have discovered how our lives are pulled between two opposing forces. The negative zombie expects the worst. The positive adventurer expects the best. Your life is determined by whichever force is dominating your mind-set at any given time. The kind of life you have is determined by the outcome of this power struggle. The tools you have to tip the balance of power are your thoughts, your actions and your smart phone. You literally hold in your hands the power to quieten your inner zombie and unlock the far-reaching potential of your inner adventurer.

In Part Two you will learn techniques to counter your inner zombie's ability to rise up again and again as one of the living dead. You will develop strategies to thwart your inner zombie every time it places its clammy hands around your hopes and dreams.

PART ONE: KEY IDEAS
Understand the power struggle inside

i. The powerful force at work in all our lives is the Universal Law of Attraction, the natural law governed by our thoughts and actions.

ii. There are two forces within you, the negative thinking inner zombie and the positive thinking inner adventurer.

iii. Your inner zombie is that part of you focusing on lack and limitation. Your inner adventurer focuses on unlimited potential and positive change. There is a battle between these two sides for control of the way you think. For the majority of people, the inner zombie wins all too often.

iv. Giving power to your inner zombie attracts the worst situations and experiences in life, but by giving power to your inner adventurer you will attract the best.

v.   Your inner zombie thrives on solemnity. When you re-skill yourself in the forgotten art of playfulness, you connect more closely to the energy of your inner adventurer.

vi.   Think and act 'as if' in order to get what you want. Adventurers effortlessly expect the outcome they desire. Their expectation is relaxed and confident but they are never attached to that outcome. Zombies fear that they won't get what they want. They are needily attached to the outcome. They inadvertently work against themselves attracting more reasons to need rather than receive. Therefore, by the Law of Attraction, the outcome remains forever out of reach.

vii.   Your smart phone is a powerful tool to help you embed a positive adventurer mind-set.

viii. Use your smart phone to develop a portfolio of words and phrases to help you focus your expectations positively. Look at these often throughout the day. Your phone is a valuable resource because it's always to hand.

ix. Use the ideas in this book so that your own story of the zombie, the adventurer and the smart phone is one where the adventurer increasingly wins through.

PART TWO

DEFEAT THE ZOMBIE INSIDE

Your inner zombie shuffles through life, moaning and groaning about everything that's wrong without taking action to put it right. Often you are giving power to your inner zombie without knowing it. This is because you have been raised, since first memory, on stories of fear, lack and limited expectations. Parents and guardians aim to keep children safe. One of the simplest ways to do this is to encourage children to be wary, using cautionary tales. These messages from our formative years can give rise to a fear-filled inner narrative that hangs over into adulthood. It's important to challenge this narrative otherwise it will undermine our ability to attract the experiences we really want.

Imagine, for a moment, your life is a film or television show. Notice how the script has been written. In the struggle between the inner zombie and the inner adventurer, many people have given the zombie the upper hand. Life becomes all about what might go wrong, how likely failure is, how important caution is, how undeserving you are, how imminent and insurmountable the risks and dangers really are. But if you understand the principles of Universal Mind and the Law of Attraction, you can become the director and screenwriter of what happens in your life. You can write a more prominent part for your inner adventurer as your life show progresses. Your inner zombie could become a minor character, making increasingly rare appearances, if you use your power as screenwriter to shape the story more positively.

When we work with an understanding of the Law of Attraction, one thing quickly becomes apparent: changes do not appear overnight. We need to shape our thoughts positively on a regular basis.

We need to sustain our efforts over time. The Law of Attraction will not be activated if we apply ourselves in a piecemeal way, lose interest, or abandon our efforts. We each need to create a manageable daily routine of adventurer thinking. We need to follow this routine religiously so that it becomes a way of life. We need to be emphatic in our actions because one of our greatest enemies is half-heartedness.

Consider the principles of weight training again. When a bodybuilder lifts weights as part of a regular training regime, she or he will notice small changes at first. These first signs of success encourage the bodybuilder to continue working towards her or his ultimate physical goal.

This principle is also true with changing your thoughts and actions. Notice how your experiences begin to change in small ways. Continue with your daily work. Over time, your entire life will begin to change too. You will attract better circumstances into your life and so become more confident of your ability to manifest positive change.

It took me from 2008 to 2014 to manifest important changes in my life and some aspects are still works in progress. There is no quick fix. But this is not necessarily a bad thing. The term 'quick fix' suggests making repairs without thorough preparation and settling for results that are rapid but not durable.

ADVENTURER AFFIRMATIONS

Adventurer affirmations can be great preparation for far-reaching and durable changes in your life. They are an effective way of changing your mind-set from focusing on risk and lack to focusing on opportunity and expansion. They are the quickest way to muzzle your inner zombie and amplify the voice of your inner adventurer. An adventurer affirmation is a short sentence describing something about your life that you want to be true. Adventurer affirmations are best written in the present tense to convey a sense of immediacy. Keep your affirmations simple and describe your end goal. Avoid describing the process. This gives the Universe the freedom it needs to find the best solutions on your behalf. Good adventurer affirmations for relationships are, 'Interesting and thoughtful people want to spend time with me.' 'My perfect partner is on his way to me.' 'I have met my ideal partner.'

Make a list of your affirmations. In your mind say each affirmation three times over as often as you can throughout the day. I often say my affirmations in the shower, walking in the street, washing my hands or waiting in queues.

A clever woman once told me how she started each day positively. Every morning as she got out of bed, she would clap her hands and say out loud, 'Today is an amazing day.' If the first words you speak each morning are positive, they set the tone for your whole day. You can say any phrase you like. The most important thing is to feel it and believe it. Paying lip service to the idea has no power. It is belief that shapes the reality we perceive.

When I realised that my job had the potential to overwhelm me, I identified how I wanted things to be different. I would get out of bed in the morning and say to myself, 'Everyone I encounter is supportive and I always get my work done in the allotted time.' The more I made these adventurer affirmations, the more I found I engaged with helpful and co-operative people at work and the less I had to work late. If anyone was difficult, I simply continued my positive focus. I thanked them silently for teaching me valuable lessons. They were helping me learn how to be patient, how to rise above my own negative emotions. If I had given in to anger, I would have awakened my inner zombie allowing it to rise up and moan, 'People are always difficult.' Getting angry would only attract more reasons to be angry – more difficult people into my experience. By contrast, my non-aggressive, approach meant the possibility of difficult encounters became increasingly remote. The difficulties I had faced in my professional role dissipated because I added no fuel to the fire of negative emotion. Be grateful for everything you are learning from a situation. Always ask, 'What is this teaching me? How do I choose the most appropriate thoughts to bring about the experiences I want in my life?'

Our lives are complex. They also have infinite potential. There may be many elements we want to change. It can be helpful to work with an array of affirmations. We can assign an affirmation to each element of change we want to see and use it to promote positive transformation in that area. Repeating affirmations throughout the day, day after day, brings about subconscious change. This affects your conscious belief system and shapes your conscious reality.

You can use your smart phone to support your work with adventurer affirmations. I used my phone's voice memo function to record myself reading a set of affirmations. This took no more than a couple of minutes. I chose, 'Everyone I encounter is supportive. I always get my work done in the allotted time. An abundance of good flows to me constantly. I am confident and self-assured.' I repeated each affirmation in the set three times, and the whole set five times. I listened to my recording whenever my mind was in a passive and receptive state. This was usually during routine tasks like dusting, shopping, exercising, waiting for trains. I found there was a particular power in hearing my own voice speak my affirmations and affirming those things I wanted to be true.

When you start working with recorded affirmations, I suggest you begin with no more than three in the set. Expand the set later as you become more familiar with the process. Listen to the recording of your adventurer affirmations on those occasions when your mind is open and receptive. Identify all of those in-between times when you might otherwise be daydreaming or thinking negatively and listen to your recording instead.

START THE DAY WITH A SENSE OF ADVENTURE

The media deliver a barrage of bad news every morning. They work on the principle that bad news sells. This may be true but it is counter productive if you want to begin your day positively.

I found it invaluable to place a ban on early morning TV and radio. Instead I chose to listen to uplifting music. This put me in the most favourable frame of mind for attracting a day filled with supportive people and rewarding experiences. I chose music without lyrics so that I was free to focus on my own ideas for the day rather than being influenced by words that were not my own.

I chose tunes that were vibrant, light and uplifting. I downloaded the Karaoke versions rather than the original songs. I made up a playlist of those tunes on my smart phone and listened each morning with the playlist set to shuffle. I danced around the kitchen making my tea and cereal and I felt optimistic even if it was windy, rainy and dark outside. I wanted to start my day feeling upbeat. I wanted to start with a sense that life was a wonderful adventure. This had a profound impact. Things would be better throughout the day, from dodging a sudden downpour, to getting through all my emails at work. The simple act of setting out in a positive adventuresome frame of mind each morning attracted experiences that matched the positive vibration of my thoughts. Choose whatever music shapes your mood in an uplifting way. It may be jazz, opera, classical, pop or chakra chants. The actual music doesn't matter, only the effect it has on you.

YOUR INNER ZOMBIE FEEDS ON 'WHAT IF'

Worry almost always takes the form of 'what if'. 'What if this doesn't work out or what if that terrible event occurs?' The 'what if' element is the root cause of our unease because it speaks of what cannot be predicted or controlled. But there are always two sides to every 'what if'. In a misguided attempt to keep you safe, your inner zombie will always encourage you to focus on what might go wrong. Counter its negative assertions by asking what would happen if things went right. Your zombie will say, 'What if you never find your perfect partner and end up on your own?' But you can choose to say to yourself instead, 'What if I meet my perfect partner and live happily ever after?' Your zombie will ask, 'What if you get ill when you get older?' But you can choose to say to yourself instead, 'What if I get older and my doctor is amazed at how healthy I am?' Concentrate on the feeling of warmth generated in your solar plexus when you assert the best possible future for yourself. In truth any outcome is possible. Misfortune is not guaranteed.

THE LESSON TO BE LEARNED WHENEVER YOUR INNER ZOMBIE RISES UP

You're working well with the Law of Attraction. You're conscientious about saying your affirmations. You're starting your day with a bad news ban. You're listening to uplifting music to shape your mood positively. And yet, you may still experience challenges with negativity. This is because your inner zombie has the unfortunate ability to rise up from the dead at any moment. Imagine any classic zombie B-movie. Just when we think our heroes have defeated the zombies, up they get – unhelpfully undead - and the heroes have to do battle with them all over again.

I had been applying the principles of the Law of Attraction for a number of years. This work had manifested decisive changes in my life.

I had my perfect partner. I was meeting interesting and influential people. I was going to exciting places and events. I had a job I loved and great work-life balance. In spite of these conclusive results, I came to learn that I had to remain vigilant. My inner zombie could still cause mischief saying things like, 'You are out of your league. You are out of your depth. It's beginning to show. Don't get used to this life. It could all end tomorrow.'

I was going out to dinner with my husband and we were being driven by his chauffeur. This was new to me and admittedly I was enjoying the experience. Every time we stopped at traffic lights, people would glance at the car wondering who we were.

After twenty minutes, we arrived at our friends' house in Battersea. Our driver got out and opened the door for my husband. My inner zombie leapt up and said, 'You can't put that chauffeur to the trouble of opening the door on your side as well. Why don't you slide across the back seat?' I was unsure what to do. Should I slide across? Should I open the door on my side? Too late! The driver was already opening the door for me.

'Thank you,' I said sheepishly and climbed out. When we arrived home later that evening, the driver opened my husband's door as before. Directed by my inner zombie, I slid across the back seat and followed my husband out of the car. Our chauffeur looked a little startled. 'I've come out on this side!' I said. I wanted to make it clear I was saving him trouble.

Later, I discussed my misgivings with my husband. He told me two important things. Firstly, opening the door for you is part of the service a chauffeur provides. Secondly, chauffeurs take pride in their professionalism so it is discourteous to prevent them from completing an aspect of their work. I was determined to disregard my inner zombie next time I was driven. I decided there was no room for zombies in our chauffeur-driven car.

Most of us can find examples where our inner zombie has reappeared in our lives. It whispers negative assertions. It makes us feel illegitimate. It tells us we are not good enough. We are not deserving of success or proper treatment. It thrives on dishing out doubt. It undermines us by questioning, 'Who do you think you really are?'

We all fall victim to our inner zombie sometimes. When it happens to you, don't criticise yourself. Watch how your zombie operates. Learn how better to respond when it hands out doubt. Be ready to fight back with an adventurer affirmation, 'I am good enough and can expect to be treated in the right way.'

In any unfamiliar situation it's easy to feel like a fish out of water. We believe we're not worthy of attention or interest. It's all too easy to think things like, 'I'm not clever enough. I'm just not worth it.' Your inner zombie will happily chime in with ideas like, 'People shouldn't go to any trouble just for you. You'd better not inconvenience anybody.' If you think you don't deserve to be treated properly, then this will become true for you. You will be overlooked. By the Law of Attraction, you will encounter situations that reinforce this internal narrative.

Your inner zombie is artful. You need to stay one step ahead. The essential quality of your inner zombie is its ability to rise up repeatedly. It's critical to remain vigilant. You are equal in status to any other person. You are as important and worthwhile as anyone. It is necessary to affirm to yourself, 'I am worthwhile and deserving.'

One evening a friend suggested that I might coach him on how to use the Law of Attraction. I had been studying a coaching course at the time and was halfway through the course work. Because I hadn't completed the whole course, I felt inadequate to the task. Your inner zombie always thrives on the idea of illegitimacy, on the idea that you have insufficient authority. Your zombie will tell you that you cannot step into a new walk of life without a formal qualification. You need a certificate in your hand. It's what people expect.

This is true for certain careers but not for all. In point of fact, I was already well qualified with a background in advisory work and holistic therapy. However, I took no notice of the facts because my inner zombie had already taken control of my narrative. I turned hesitantly to my friend and said, 'I can't coach you yet, I'm only halfway through my course.' Down went my self-esteem and my aspirations in a single sentence. This is why continual vigilance is so important. Your inner zombie has no right to hijack your narrative. Don't let it get away with it.

With vigilance, I could have managed the situation more effectively. I could have wrestled control of the narrative back from my inner zombie. I could have said to my friend, 'I would love to coach you. I have some great ideas we could share. I'm only halfway through my coaching course, but I'm very happy that we work together, if you are.'

Vigilance is so important because your inner zombie is always lurking in the background. It can even hijack your narrative without your realising it. Be attentive to your thoughts and make sure they really are your own. Be ready to counter your inner zombie's influence by reframing the narrative affirmatively. Stay sharp because the B-movie zombie always returns. Don't let it get the better of you in the sequel.

THE ZOMBIE DANCE

In the day-to-day challenges of life, it's easy to lose positive focus. We realise half way through the day that we have allowed our inner zombie to be in control the majority of the time. We become stressed. We encounter challenges. We find ourselves thinking too much about what we don't want. We are in danger of losing heart and momentum. Our inner self-talk can deteriorate to the extent that we become disconnected from our genuine desires. This is when it is essential to confront your inner zombie head on. You need to take back the initiative decisively.

I was experiencing a challenging time at work. I felt trapped in unbreakable cycles of effort and failure. As I was getting ready for work one morning, I found my mind wandering into dangerous territory. I was focusing exclusively on worst-case scenarios – performance targets that could never be achieved and my boss venting his frustrations on me and my colleagues. I stopped myself and asked the question, 'Whose narrative is this?' I brought my awareness into the moment looking at my soapy face in the shaving mirror. I realised these were the thoughts of my inner zombie and they were damaging my chances of overcoming the challenges at work. I realised I had to take definitive action. Awareness is always the first point of power. It is essential to be aware of what's going on before you can change what's going on.

I put my razor down. I stuck my arms out in front of me. I rolled my eyes. I moaned and groaned like the quintessential horror movie zombie. This farcical zombie dance radically altered the tone of the moment. The absurdity of the dance revealed the absurdity of my inner zombie. The more I danced, the more I realised how absurd life can be. If a meteor hit the earth, no one would care about performance targets or difficult bosses! Playing with absurdity reveals a molehill where we believed a mountain once stood.

The zombie dance had exposed my negative mind-set for what it was. It freed me to see instead everything I was grateful for. It freed me to reconnect with my inner adventurer. I noticed how sunny it was outside. I noticed the aroma of freshly brewing coffee in my home. I noticed my gratitude for plentiful, hot running water. I remembered I was meeting up with a close friend that evening. I felt the warmth of that friendship and was grateful for it. I was choosing to be aware of the good things in life. I began to feel uplifted.

My inner zombie had returned within as little as ten minutes. I had started to think about my work frustrations again. But this time I was better prepared. I did my zombie dance again.

Once more, I was diminishing the power of my inner zombie through ridicule and I realised suddenly that I was having fun doing it. Throughout the day I continued to dance, making sure I found a quiet place to do so. If that wasn't possible I simply pictured myself doing the zombie dance in my mind's eye. This had a similarly uplifting effect. My mind-set became more positive. I felt closer to my inner adventurer and I was able to bring much more positive experiences to me. By the end of the day, my overworked boss had even sent me three complimentary emails.

With practice, this zombie dance has enabled me to close down negative self-talk. Next time you realise your inner zombie has taken control of your own narrative, take away its power using the power of ridicule. Invent your own preposterous dance to humiliate and silence your inner zombie. Then take stock of all the good things around you. Use your awareness of those good things to reaffirm to yourself that life is a wonderful adventure.

Everyone has experienced a zombie attack in the small hours of the morning. We lie in the dark unable to sleep because of concerns about finances, work, relationships or whatever else is worrying us. Even though it may not seem like it, this is the perfect time to bring out your zombie dance. Move your limbs zombie style as you lie in bed. It may feel quite strange at first. But this zombie dance will banish doom-laden nighttime worries. As you ape your inner zombie, your negative thoughts begin to subside. It becomes easier to focus instead on the good things in your life. Cast your mind towards the coming sunrise. Picture the sunlight that will soon be streaming into your home. Savour the promise of hot buttered toast and freshly made tea. Imagine the adventure of a new day. Very soon your inner zombie will be defeated and shuffle away towards the far horizon.

Worrying about a situation is not improving that situation. It is never constructive. It is always self-sabotage. Absurdity helps take the sting out of worry. Laugh and your troubles are automatically diminished. Then you can approach any situation with clearer perspective and from a position of greater strength.

INSPIRATIONAL WALLPAPER

Type a positive word or phrase into Google images. Let's suppose you type the word 'happiness'. The search engine will find 'happiness' presented in a variety of typefaces and colours against different backgrounds. Download your favourite design and save it in a folder on your smart phone. I made a folder titled 'Inspirational' and collected well over a hundred images of words and phrases that appealed to me including 'Joy', 'Success', 'Today is a great day', 'You are fantastic', 'Damn you, gorgeous', 'You are great' and so on. Each morning I opened the folder and chose at random a positive statement for the day. I set that statement as my smart phone's wallpaper. Every time I looked at my phone, the first thing I saw was that inspirational wallpaper.

How many times do you look at your phone in one day? Ten, twenty, thirty times or more? This means you will see your inspirational wallpaper ten, twenty, thirty times or more a day. Regular exposure to the affirmative statement reinforces your relationship with it. This repetition embeds the positive thought in your subconscious. This is what makes it such a powerful practice.

I was newly divorced. I was living at my father's house and beginning to explore the London social scene. I had joined a gay men's dining club with the aim of making new friends and maybe meeting someone special. I always felt nervous going to meet new people particularly if there was the potential for a romantic connection. I was going to my first dining club event and had chosen 'Damn you, gorgeous' as my smart phone's wallpaper. I looked at it several times on my way to the restaurant and it felt funny but fun. Every time I looked at this wallpaper, I also thought to myself, 'I am attractive and worthy of attention.' My inner zombie tried to undermine me by saying, 'Who do you think you are? No-one will be interested in you when there will be so many other attractive and charismatic people there.' But I stood firm. I repeated my affirmation, 'I am attractive and worthy of attention.' I made a point of checking my phone regularly. I wanted to see over and over again the words 'Damn you, gorgeous'. I went into the restaurant and joined the dining club group for drinks before dinner. I was approached by a charming fellow diner and we talked for a while about our respective travels in Europe. I was enjoying the conversation when I was tapped on the shoulder by another club member. He introduced himself and asked if this was my first dinner event. Gradually it dawned on me that these two bright and sociable men were competing with each other for my attention. I smiled to myself as I glanced down briefly at my phone and saw the prophetic words 'Damn you, gorgeous'.

AN ARMY OF ZOMBIES

We have focused our attention so far on the zombie inside *you*. We have identified its tendency to rise up just when you think it's been defeated once and for all. We've established the consequent need for constant vigilance. Now we have to acknowledge that you are not the only one with an inner zombie. Everyone has an inner zombie which means there is an entire army of zombies at large in the world.

It's easy to recognise when people are acting under the influence of their inner zombies. They will be negative and critical, focusing predominantly on problems, challenges, difficult people and controversy. It's important not to judge. People are often under the influence of their inner zombies unwittingly. Always remember that the negative things people say are not the truth. They have no power over you unless you give them power. Social pressure to conform can also encourage people to complain together. This behaviour can create seductive feelings of belonging but it is founded on a treacherous principle. We are enticed to say together, 'Haven't we all got it bad?' This negative energy fuels the inner zombie in us all. The army gets stronger. Many of us will try to fit in with the prevailing negative tone, attempting to outdo each other by describing greater and greater calamities. We allow our inner zombies free rein in order not to feel excluded from the group. The army gets stronger still. The English actress and cult figure Fenella Fielding once said, 'People are very free with their bad advice.' People are just as free with their negative opinions. Your inner zombie will always side with other zombies. People under the control of their inner zombies will expect you to agree with them. By the Law of Attraction they are bringing negative situations into their lives and they want your company. These people are not trying to be deliberately unkind. They're simply adrift. They have allowed their inner zombie to take control of their thinking. They're being duped into focusing on what's bad rather than good, on what's going wrong rather than right. They are in a sinking ship. It's taking on water and about to capsize in an ocean of woe. Don't get onboard.

Some people may even believe it's an act of kindness to emphasise a negative point of view. They believe they are alerting you to the potential pitfalls in life. They want to protect you from, or prepare you for, what they believe to be life's inevitable disappointments. They believe they are helping you to 'toughen up'. But this is immensely misguided. Remember Fenella's words, 'People are very free with their bad advice.' Anticipating calamity is no way to prepare for life. Dwelling on negativity only serves to attract negative experiences. If someone really wants to help you, they will encourage you to build up your resilience to negative influences. What you really need in life is a negativity blocker. If you are a Star Trek fan this will be easy. Whenever someone says something negative like, 'It's so hard to get a promotion isn't it? There's so much competition.' Say to yourself, 'Raise shields!' This is a statement of your determination not to allow that negative idea to influence your narrative. You are declaring your right to remain immune. Use any quick and memorable phrase that works for you. You might say, 'Close flood gates,' or 'Not true for me,' or even, 'Zombie back in your box!' Experiment with different phrases until you find the one that resonates most powerfully with you. When you neutralise the negativity of other people's inner zombies, you also protect yourself from your own.

EMOTIONAL TURBULENCE

If you encounter someone in a bad temper, it's easy to assume they are angry because of you. But there can be any number of reasons for someone's turbulent mood. Difficulties at home or at work may have put them in a negative frame of mind. Your inner adventurer knows to stand to one side. Assess the situation dispassionately. It is most likely that you are neither the cause nor can you be the solution. If you do react to emotional turbulence, you risk contributing to it further. You can make matters worse for the person in a negative state of mind and yourself. You risk operating from a standpoint of fear – that somehow you are responsible for the other person's negative state. You risk waking up your own inner zombie and carrying someone else's negativity around with you for the rest of the day. The voice of your inner adventurer will always counsel you to feel compassion towards others experiencing difficulty. Operate from a standpoint of love. See turbulence for what it is. But remain centred in your own reality. You can feel compassion for the other person while focusing on the good you have in your own life.

Emotional turbulence can also arise from the false sense that someone else's thoughtlessness is a deliberate and personal affront to you.

One New Year's Eve, my next door neighbour threw a lively party that went on until six o'clock in the morning. Although it was New Year's Eve, it was nevertheless thoughtless to disturb the neighbourhood with loud music for such a long time. I lost an entire night's sleep. I felt exhausted the whole of the following day and robbed of the chance to enjoy the holiday. I could have stirred up inner emotional turbulence about the situation. I could have allowed my inner zombie to tell me that the noise disturbance was an attack on me personally rather than an example of thoughtlessness with no intended target. I could have obsessed about the injustice of it all.

Instead, I made a conscious choice to take a step back. I decided to try to forgive the mistake that had been made. I felt better immediately because I had resisted the temptation to embroil myself in emotional turbulence that would not serve me. I understood that the choice to forgive meant I was indicating to Universal Mind that I wanted to live in a world where forgiveness was the norm, not retribution. Through the Law of Attraction, my act of forgiving would, in turn, attract forgiveness to me the next time I made a mistake.

GETTING THE VERY BEST OUT OF YOUR INTERACTIONS WITH OTHER PEOPLE

If your friend, colleague or partner is difficult or negative, you can't force them to change. You have no real power to change anybody else. Only they can make change happen. External changes occur when someone makes a conscious internal agreement with themselves to change. Your only power lies in altering the way you, yourself, regard and react to another person. You can choose to appreciate, and focus on, the positive aspects of any relationship.

Suppose you are having a challenging time with a person in your life. Put a picture of that person on your phone and look at it often throughout the day. Each time you look at the picture, think of a character trait you admire. Think of more good qualities and make a list of these on your phone. Look at the list regularly to remind yourself of these likeable traits.

The person's negative characteristics will still be there but when you choose to focus instead on someone's positive traits you are sending a signal to Universal Mind that you want to experience more of those better qualities. Whenever you are with that person, this will be your experience.

One of my bosses, a very senior manager, was notoriously difficult. He shouted at, and humiliated, many members of staff including colleagues close to me. He was so intimidating that even a senior member of staff was reduced to tears. Another colleague trembled and stuttered whenever he came near. This was unnerving but I did not allow my inner zombie to profit from the situation. I chose to focus on my boss's good traits. He was a bully but I chose to remind myself that he always praised efficiency and felt passionately about safeguarding our jobs. He had brought coherence and clarity of purpose to our department where previously there had been confusion and lack of direction. I told myself how grateful I was for these developments and I affirmed to myself that I only ever had positive experiences with him. I wrote down a positive character assessment of my boss and stored it on my phone. I looked at it repeatedly each working day. My colleagues continued to experience bullying from him in the work place. Our organisation took steps to develop my boss's interpersonal skills. My colleagues would relate stories about his latest aggressive behaviour. I tried to be as supportive as possible. I agreed how distressing it must be but I didn't join in the chorus of criticism. I declined to sign up to a contract binding me to a future of negative experiences with my boss.

Instead I would say, 'I haven't found him to be like that with me. That hasn't been my experience of him.' I then re-iterated to myself those good points about him listed on my phone. I felt grateful that he was always courteous and encouraging to me. Throughout my time in the department, I never experienced the controlling side of his character. I was the only person able to say this.

We often hear parents, carers and teachers tell children, 'If you can't say something nice about someone, don't say anything at all.' This may sound simplistic but it describes a fundamental principle of the Law of Attraction. Universal Mind will manifest whatever you focus your attention on. If you focus on the negative in others, you will attract more of those negative qualities. That is what you are asking the Universe for.

It can be tempting to react rashly to a difficult person. If we allow ourselves to be provoked by others we give our power away. We hand over control to others whenever we lose control of ourselves. When we choose our reactions wisely, we assume control of our lives. Each of us can shape our experiences consciously by choosing our own thoughts, words and actions with care. We hold all the cards. We are independent of others. We have all the power. Informed use of that power enables us to take steps to identify and silence the voice of our inner zombie. By managing our thoughts selectively we can unlock the potential of our inner adventurer.

YOUR INNER ZOMBIE FEEDS ON GOSSIP

People dominated by their inner zombies gossip. Gossip is one of the surest signs of an inner zombie at work. Gossip is a powerful means of amplifying negative thought among a group people. It's very easy to be seduced into joining in. It can feel safe and exciting to be 'in on the gossip'. But gossip is always poisonous. Someone always gets hurt in the end. The only effective defence is to approach life like a skilful lawyer making judgments based exclusively on hard evidence.

I was looking forward to meeting up with a relatively new friend when he was next in London. I really enjoyed spending time with him and we had agreed to meet when a business trip next brought him to town. I emailed him to ask when he would be coming. No reply. My inner zombie hauled itself up out of the earth and told me, 'He doesn't really want to see you. You've probably upset him in some way.' I continued to wait and my inner zombie continued to sow seeds of doubt in my mind. 'He's clearly not a very reliable person,' my zombie said. 'There are so few genuine people around these days.' I felt a tinge of doubt. Was my new friend ignoring me? I wondered if I had done anything wrong. Maybe he was just being polite when he had said he wanted to meet. I wasn't interesting enough to warrant his friendship.

Three weeks later, he emailed to tell me the date he would be in London. He said how much he was looking forward to catching up. He hadn't emailed me sooner because he hadn't had a firm date for his visit. He'd had nothing concrete to tell me. See how damaging it can be to form a negative conclusion based on conjecture. People have lots of different ways of dealing with text or email. Some people will simply not respond unless they have something meaningful to say. Some will be very slow at responding to any message. Others will reply instantly. None of these approaches is right or wrong, they're just different. Give control of your narrative to your inner zombie and you will be plagued by doubt about the motivations of others. Give control to your inner adventurer and you will attract reasons to see the best in everybody.

This chapter has explored ways to confront and vanquish the zombie within *you* and to protect yourself against the zombies in others. There is an army of shuffling zombies out there waiting to overwhelm you with ideas of limitation and lack. Stay vigilant because the next zombie attack can happen at any time.

PART TWO: KEY IDEAS
Silence your inner zombie

i.   Picture your life as a film or TV show. All too often your inner zombie has control of the script. But in truth, you are the director and scriptwriter of what happens in your life. Take back control. Write your inner zombie a smaller and smaller part and increase the role of your inner adventurer as your life show progresses.

ii. It's necessary to invest time and effort to manifest positive changes in your life. This work is not a quick fix. Take time to develop your adventurer mind-set and you will get the life you want in the end.

iii. Use adventurer affirmations to change your mind-set and attract more rich and rewarding experiences into your life. Record your affirmations using the voice memo function on your smart phone and listen to them over and over again.

iv.   Difficult people and situations are learning opportunities. They allow you to practice managing your responses. When you choose to adopt a positive response to any situation you will manifest the happiest possible outcome.

v.   Avoid listening to the news in the morning. Listen instead to uplifting tunes to start your morning positively and see every day as an adventure.

vi.   Protect yourself from people in the clutches of their own inner zombies. Raise shields against their negative ideas.

vii. Emotional turbulence can arise from the false sense that someone else's thoughtlessness is a deliberate and personal affront to you. Make a conscious choice to step back. Choose to be forgiving of thoughtlessness and you will, in turn, attract forgiveness for your own mistakes.

viii. You cannot force another person to change but you can choose to place your attention on the best things about that person. You will see more of these best qualities as a result. Use the notes and wallpaper functions on your phone to help you.

ix. We tell children, 'If you can't say something nice about someone, don't say anything at all.' This simple motto touches on a fundamental principle of the Law of Attraction so it's sound advice for adults too.

x. Our inner zombie wants us to assume the worst in any given situation particularly when evaluating the actions of others. By contrast adventurers base their opinions on hard evidence. Apply this rule in your own life and never judge others on hearsay or gossip.

PART THREE

YOU ARE A BORN ADVENTURER

Your inner zombie is waiting to turn any challenge or problem to its advantage. It is waiting to wrest control of your narrative from you. Whenever your zombie does manage to take control, you can choose to regard it as a learning opportunity. Notice how you became aware of the shift in the narrative. Experiment with different approaches to retaking control. This combination of awareness and action will enable you to silence your inner zombie and hand back control to your inner adventurer.

Connecting with your inner adventurer is not about feeling aggressive or arrogant. Nor is it about conforming to stereotypes regarding confidence, looks or charisma. (Your inner adventurer appreciates the profusion of positive qualities in all people.) Authentic connection with your inner adventurer occurs when you feel worthy of the richness life has to offer. Only through this profound feeling of worth can you realise your true potential. You rise to a level of awareness where your expectation of a better future is lightly but firmly held. There is no fear. There is no doubt. In this state you become a conscious agent of the Law of Attraction. This chapter will explore ways to help you connect authentically with your inner adventurer and further amplify the adventurer's good influence.

Work with an 'abundance buddy'. An abundance buddy is someone who shares your interest in the Law of Attraction. Go on the journey together, sharing ideas, supporting each other when the work gets difficult and celebrating each other's successes. Working with a buddy can help you achieve much more than working alone. There is no need to put an advert in the local paper. As you start to use the Law of Attraction to improve your life, more and more people will appear in your life who are familiar with the Law and the power of Universal Mind. One of these people will be your abundance buddy.

Every week I have a one-hour check-in with my buddy. We talk to each other about successes and challenges and help each other with suggestions and encouragement. If you can't meet face-to-face then you can call, FaceTime or Skype at an agreed time, or check in via email. It's fun to bounce ideas off a like-minded individual and it really works. You support and inspire each other. You learn from each other's experiences and avoid making similar mistakes. You become more certain of manifesting the changes you want. You explore together the reasons for any setbacks. You share ideas about focusing your thoughts and feelings in the most advantageous way to face any upcoming challenges. You can continue to support each other throughout the week by sending a positive affirmation each day via text message. Choose an affirmation for something that you really want to improve in your life and share it with your buddy. Ask your buddy to send you a text of your affirmation at different times each day. This will help you focus on what you want to attract into your life. It will also remind you that you are not alone in your endeavours.

A COMMUNITY OF POSITIVITY

As you and your abundance buddy develop your work with the Law Of Attraction, you will meet more people who follow similar principles. This is a great opportunity to expand your network. Instead of having just one abundance buddy you can build a whole community of positivity. This is a group of like-minded people who meet regularly each month or each quarter. Here are some helpful guidelines for setting up a group of your own. Have a theme for discussions. For example you might choose to discuss how to deal with other people's negativity. Encourage the group to share their observations and ideas. A guided conversation is easier for everyone to take part in and gives everyone something of interest to consider. For the more reticent members of your group, it can be more agreeable to work in pairs, discuss the theme and feedback to the whole group. Watch a short You Tube film on the Law of Attraction. Review an article from the internet. Agree a Law of Attraction book for the group to discuss (just like a book club). These activities will help to move your conversation forward. Different people can take turns to host the group meetings. Building your community of positivity is enjoyable and enables you to support, and be supported by, others on your journey.

ACT LIKE AN ADVENTURER

Our inner zombie sees life as rigid and fixed. It tells us it is safest to be constrained by other people's expectations and requirements. We should always know our place. We should never put anyone out. By contrast, an adventurer sees the world as a flexible and fluid place to be investigated, experimented with and enjoyed.

You're looking at a restaurant menu and a dish of fresh linguine catches your eye. The only trouble is the linguine is served with crab. You're not fond of crab but you see baked salmon elsewhere on the menu. Salmon linguine is what you would really like. Your inner zombie will say, 'But that's not on the menu.' It will suggest that you shouldn't put the restaurant to any trouble.

'Somebody else might want that salmon.' It will tell you to order another dish entirely rather than risk any awkwardness and embarrassment.

Your inner adventurer will encourage you to have exactly what you want. It will encourage you to order the linguine but to add that you would prefer it with salmon. Your adventurer will encourage you to be courteous but clear with your request. The restaurant can always say no but they are most likely to say yes.

You decide who controls your narrative. Do you choose your inner zombie and self-effacement or do you choose your inner adventurer and self-determination? There's very little hardship involved if the restaurant puts salmon in your linguine instead of crab. The world won't end. No one will be hurt.

Listen to the voice of your inner adventurer and you will live a more balanced life. You will respect yourself. You will respect others. And they will respect you. The voice of your inner adventurer would never counsel you to be domineering or dismissive of others. This would only serve to bring domineering and dismissive people into your experience. Your inner adventurer will always counsel being gracious and kind to others. This is the way to receive graciousness and kindness in return. This is the Law of Attraction reflecting back to us the behaviours we express in the world.

When we change the way we think, we begin to change the nature of our life experiences. Approach life from the position of the shuffling zombie and you will attract awkward and uncomfortable situations. Approach life from the position of the self-determining adventurer and you will attract more relaxed and agreeable situations. You have as much right as anybody to consider yourself worthwhile and to create your life accordingly. Nowhere is it written that there is a limit to aspiration.

ACCEPT THE GIFT OF A COMPLIMENT

If we learn to feel good about ourselves we manifest more reasons to sustain that good feeling. Receiving a compliment can enhance our feelings of self-worth dramatically. This in turn increases our capacity to manifest more good feeling in our lives. But it's not in many people's natures to accept compliments easily. We think we are a better person if we are self-deprecating. This has to be an error of judgment if we believe in the Law of Attraction. The tendency to be self-deprecating illustrates the challenge many of us face when it comes to feeling genuinely worthwhile. We look at our reflection in the mirror and feel immediately inclined towards self-criticism. We give more energy to the negative aspects we perceive about ourselves and ignore our positive attributes entirely. One of the most beneficial things we can do is learn to accept a compliment with gratitude rather than embarrassment. When someone gives you a compliment, receive it graciously thinking, 'Thank you, yes I am.' Resist the temptation to refuse or deny the compliment. It does not make you a better person.

My husband once complimented a waitress on her glossy shoulder-length hair. 'Oh no, it's very straggly today,' she said. By refusing the compliment she was saying, 'That's not me. I'm not that person.' The Universe doesn't understand irony or modesty and will comply with any statement you make. By refusing the compliment about her hair she made it less likely she would be complimented about that quality in the future.

If you refuse a compliment you are refusing a gift. The giver will not be inclined to offer you another so readily in the future. When you accept the gift of a compliment with good grace, you are not being arrogant, you are being grateful. That 'yes I am' can be something you say silently to yourself. You can smile warmly and say, 'Thank you.' Then return the compliment. It's important to give gifts as well as receive them.

A friend once complimented me on a buffet I had prepared for a housewarming, 'Moon made a delicious buffet and he made it all seem so effortless.'

'Oh no,' I said. 'I just opened some packets of quiche and threw some pasta in a bowl.'

In actual fact, I had done more than just that. But my inner zombie said, 'He can't be talking about you, can he? I mean you're hardly a gourmet chef.'

Even as I refused the compliment, I recognised the voice of my inner zombie at work. Self-awareness is the critical first step to being able to change. Now I have learned to accept compliments wherever I go. And because I accept those compliments with gratitude, I experience more instances of being complimented.

Accepting compliments makes them true for you. So if someone says you are insightful and good at giving advice, saying no to that compliment means you are saying no to being insightful and good at giving advice. If you say yes to the compliment you will become more insightful and good at giving advice through the

Law of Attraction. Similarly if someone says you are charming and interesting, then saying no to that compliment means you don't want it. Universal Mind will then connect you with more and more people who find everyone else charming and interesting but not you. Accept the compliment to amplify that admirable quality in yourself.

Never throw a gift back in the face of the giver. It is ungracious and unkind. But it is also an unkindness to yourself. You are saying that you don't deserve the gift of that compliment. You are stating to the Universe that you are not good enough. It is far better for all concerned if you accept the compliment and say silently to yourself, 'Thank you. Yes I am. This is true for me.'

BOOST YOUR CONFIDENCE WITH THE HELP OF YOUR SMART PHONE

As well as accepting compliments, it is really helpful to keep a record of them. This can easily be done using your phone. Simply set up a new page in your phone's notes function and call it 'How others see me'.

Every time you receive a positive comment such as, 'You always take a great picture,' or 'You are so kind and so clever,' make a note of it on your 'How others see me' page. Next to the comment, put the name of the person who said it. Take time out of your day to stop and look at these positive observations about you. The action of focusing on the list will raise your level of positive consciousness about your own value. Through Universal Mind this will attract more reasons to feel great about yourself and the life you're living.

This practice can help you to reshape your self-image positively. It can remind you of all the good qualities that others see in you. How quickly do we forget or dismiss the compliments others give us? On the other hand, if someone says something negative we take it on board and accept it as a destructive truth. It provides ammunition for our inner zombie. It becomes the foundation for those negative comments our inner zombie loves, 'Be more successful? Get your perfect partner? Who do you think you are?' Now you can use your list of compliments to refute any claim made by your zombie. Put your energy and emotion into loving and believing in yourself and the Law of Attraction will bring you a life full of love and self-belief.

Whenever you make a decision or respond to different events in your life, always stop and check who is in control of your inner narrative. Is your narrative based on fear and lack or is it based on love and expansiveness? Imagine you decide to change your wardrobe and adopt a different look. Do you think about all the ways other people might criticise you? Or do you imagine the compliments you might receive? The first state of mind arises from fear, the second from love and a belief in the benevolence of life.

My husband is an artist. We were going to private views at art galleries regularly and I was enjoying the creative freedom and eccentricity of the London art scene. I wanted to develop a new style of my own. I decided to start wearing hats even though my shyness had prevented me from wearing them before. Just the thought of a woolly hat for the winter had filled me with embarrassment. But the art scene felt different. It was removed from my everyday life. It gave me the opportunity to experiment with who I could be and different ways of presenting myself. It felt like an open and safe environment. The more I experimented, the more confident I became. I received compliments for my new look and accepted them graciously. I decided to integrate my new look into my everyday life by wearing a hat to a friend's drinks party. I felt a little cautious about taking my 'art world dressing up' into my wider social life but wanted to see what the reaction would be like.

My friends said nothing.

I told myself that this did not constitute a negative reaction. I chose to think instead that they were in awe of my new style. After about an hour, one of them finally said to me, 'So, what's with the hat then?'

'Oh, the hat thing?' I said. 'I just thought I'd do something mad today.' My confidence collapsed. I imagined a criticism where perhaps none was intended. I had fallen into the trap of being defensive. I had allowed my inner zombie to take control of my narrative. 'Who do you think you are in that ridiculous hat?'

Had my inner adventurer been in control, I would have said, 'I've discovered I absolutely love hats. I want to wear them more and more. I'm even thinking of wearing this hat in bed.'

Picture the people you admire who have a distinctive style of their own. Know that you are part of that community. You are not alone. Any conscious choice you make for yourself is legitimate just by virtue of its being the choice you have made. If other people choose to be part of the herd, that doesn't make their choice more legitimate than yours. It just makes them part of the herd.

You can choose to love who you are and express that identity wholeheartedly. The Universe will support you. You will attract more reasons to feel good about yourself. You will attract more reasons to feel good about the life you are living.

MARK YOURSELF UP, NOT DOWN

At a party one night, there is a man called Tristan. He is widely read, cultured and intelligent. He is chatting with another man called Mick. Mick knows that Tristan, by reputation, is clever and widely read. During the course of the conversation, Mick tries to impress on Tristan that he is equally well read. Mick asks Tristan if he has read this particular novel or if he knows that particular play. Tristan has read none of the literature Mick talks about. Tristan begins to feel more and more uncomfortable even though it is unlikely that two people would have read exactly the same novels or plays.

Later, Tristan feels he has been subjected to a game of aggressive one-upmanship. But is this true? Or was Mick so in awe of Tristan's reputation that he was merely trying keep up. Was he simply trying to conceal his own feelings of inadequacy? Quite often in situations like these we can feel like Tristan. We can assume that other people are putting us down when actually they are just trying to keep up. Think about this story again. With greater awareness, Tristan would have understood that Mick was feeling inadequate and was simply trying to impress. Instead of feeling put down, Tristan would take Mick's behaviour as a compliment.

A well-known movie actor once confided that fans would sometimes appear brusque or rude when meeting him. He understood that his fans were often nervous and excited in his presence and this explained their odd behaviour. Rather than see their brusqueness negatively, he identified it as a sign of the intensity of their feeling for him. And he was enormously grateful for their love and support. He chose not to judge the surface appearance of the situation. He took a step back and considered what was actually taking place rather than making negative assumptions. This non-judgmental thinking has ensured his continued success as one of America's most well-liked and successful actors.

When we meet someone new, many of us share a tendency to 'mark ourselves down' in comparison. All too often, we assume that new people are more knowledgeable and more confident than we are. We make these assumptions because new people are unknown quantities. Our inner zombie feeds on our insecurities, and encourages us to come to negative conclusions. If we are marking ourselves down in comparison to others, the likelihood is they are doing the same. Once we realise this, we can take a different approach. Disengage from the zombie narrative that every new person is a threat. Reframe your view of new people as potential allies and teachers.

Whenever you meet someone new, take a breath and affirm your belief in your own self-worth. Put your inner adventurer in control of your narrative. Mark yourself up, rather than down. Give your best to others and they can then give their best to you.

I often meet with a group of friends. We're all of a similar age. We share similar interests and enjoy each other's company. One evening, we were meeting for a meal and one of my friends was bringing her new partner. He was much younger than her and he seemed bored. He was not particularly talkative. He appeared restless and keen to leave at the earliest opportunity. We all assumed that he thought we were boring and old. Some time later, we learned the real reason for his initial coolness. He had seen us as worldly, experienced and confident. He had marked himself down by comparison. He felt he had insufficient life experience to interest us. He felt intimidated precisely because we were older.

It's not uncommon to feel apprehensive about the prospect of new neighbours. We wonder how problematic or difficult they might be. We rarely put ourselves in their position and imagine that they could be feeling similar anxieties. If you feel trepidation about new people, they could be feeling the same trepidation about you.

These feelings of trepidation are just another example of marking yourself down. You are visualising yourself in a negative position compared with others based on non-existent evidence. Visualise yourself, instead, in the other person's position. This is an act of empathy. Empathy is a source of strength. Empathy allows you to approach any situation from a position of greater assurance and openness. Empathy for others, ironically, is the key to marking yourself up.

By the Law of Attraction, expecting new people to be difficult will attract difficulties in your encounters with them. When you mark yourself up, you anticipate mutually beneficial experiences with all new people. It becomes easier to expect the best. Expect everyone you meet to have something of worth to share with you. The more you affirm this, the more beneficial your experiences will be.

WRITE THE SCRIPT OF YOUR OWN LIFE

We are the authors of our own lives. We have control over the events in our lives just as a television scriptwriter has control over the events in a TV show. Imagine your own life as a long-running TV series. Sometimes it can feel as if you are playing a part in an episode written by someone else. It can feel as if the storyline you really want will never be broadcast.

Because you are the author of your own life, it is possible to change the script. You can step back and ask yourself how the current series is looking. Is your show worth watching? Is it top of the ratings or is it floundering? Is it time for a rewrite? To change the script you need to change your thinking. As your internal narrative is transformed, you begin to see the potential for positive change in every aspect of life.

Begin this work by evaluating your current life story. How do the people around you support or undermine your aims? To what extent are you held back by other people's ideas of limitation and lack? To what extent are these people unable to support you because they are unwittingly dominated by their own inner zombies? It is important to have a clear understanding of who is affecting you negatively. Once you have clarity it is essential to take action. It could be better for you if certain people in your life are given less prominent roles and only make occasional guest appearances.

Are there people around you who contribute positively to your experiences but appear only infrequently in the show? Are these fellow adventurers a potential source of inspiration and reinforcement for your aims? It is important to be clear about who can help you. Once you have clarity you can act. Spend more time in the company of these adventurers. Encourage them to move from their occasional guest role to becoming full-time cast members.

When you think about your life as a script you take the emotional heat out of the changes you wish to make. If a TV show is flagging in the ratings what do the scriptwriters do? They change the storyline.

What aspects of your story support your hopes and aims for the future? What aspects of your story keep you mired in doubt? Focus only on the good aspects of your current story. Give no power to negative situations. Consider the developments you want to make in the storyline and write down statements describing these changes.

Put these new plot points on the wall opposite your bed. Every night when you go to sleep, look at them. Every morning when you wake up, look at them again. One plot point might be, 'I am meeting new and interesting friends.' Another might be, 'New career opportunities are appearing for me.' Focus on these new plot points with firm belief. Move in their direction. Accept invitations or join groups. Search the internet for career opportunities. You are setting the scene for the show of your life to develop a brand new storyline, the one that you really want to see.

BRING MORE SUPPORTIVE PEOPLE INTO YOUR LIFE

For the majority of us, our friendships and associations are formed in a haphazard way. We move into a new neighbourhood or start a new job and friendships form almost unconsciously. We rarely stop to consider if these are the friendships that serve us best. But our friendships can be developed in a more conscious way. We have the power to decide who we spend time with and how much time we spend on each friendship. Through conscious choice we can create the most positive blend of friendships and associations so that everybody benefits.

I googled the words 'Fabulous' and 'Abundance' and found a bright digital image of each. I printed them out and put them on my bathroom mirror. I then printed photos of people I knew and liked and stuck them on my mirror under categories of 'Great People', 'Helpful People' and 'Stellar People'. Finally, underneath the words and pictures I printed in big bold letters 'More Please, Thank You'. Over the next few months I found my time was increasingly taken up with the people I had described as great, helpful and stellar. The great people were always on hand with positivity and encouragement. The helpful people did things that were incredibly supportive personally and professionally. I learned wonderful life lessons from the stellar people. I made a conscious decision to exclude from my list anyone I found negative or demotivating. I diverted all my attention to visualising the great, stellar and helpful people I wanted to see more of. The Law of Attraction will always bring you more of what you focus on. Consequently I found negative and demotivating people began to appear less and less frequently in my life.

Just as we can make conscious choices about the people we have in our lives, we can make conscious choices about the situations we have in our lives. Often we accept situations without questioning their value to us. We just go along with the way things are. Any situation can be improved through conscious awareness. Examine any situation in your life and ask yourself, 'Is this part of a rich and rewarding existence?' If the answer is no then why are you doing it? What situation would suit you better? Take action to manifest change. If you want to move to a certain neighbourhood, spend lots of time in that neighbourhood. Spend time in cafes there. Meet friends for drinks or supper there. Walk around and window-shop there. If you want a certain job, buy the trade papers for that profession and have them on your coffee table. Watch documentaries and dramas centred on that profession. If appropriate, dress as if you already work in that profession. Do these things regularly and the Universe will make these situations real for you. It will act to bring your life into line with the roles you are playing. If you can't afford to stay at The Ritz, linger over a coffee there for a couple of hours. By doing so, you become the kind of person who spends time at The Ritz. This becomes true for you. But if you never even show up at The Ritz, it can never become part of your reality.

After my divorce I moved back to London. I was forty-three and living at my father's house. To make matters worse, my childhood bedroom was still decorated with jungle wallpaper. As I lay in bed at night staring at the lions and tigers, my inner zombie said, 'This is what you are reduced to. You should be grateful that you haven't lost everything. You're washed up. And as far as relationships go, everyone wants a twenty-one-year-old. No-one will be remotely interested in you.'

As that voice droned on I took a deep breath and thought to myself, 'This is not real.' I understood what my inner zombie was trying to do and that awareness gave me power. I took the conscious decision to transfer control of this narrative to my inner adventurer. I decided to feel grateful. I had hit rock bottom, so now the only way was up. I took action. I stripped the wallpaper, whitewashed the walls and began internet dating. I decided I was going to meet vibrant and interesting people. I was going to meet someone special. I was going to have a more eventful life.

I discovered that dating websites were not necessarily the best places to find a meaningful relationship. Some people were not looking for a long-term relationship. Others were already involved. Others were misleading in their profile information. I decided to try a bespoke introduction agency where a dating consultant personally matches clients according to their compatibility. This was an expensive service and I could have easily walked away. Instead I told myself that if other people were prepared to invest in this service then there was a good chance they would be serious about finding a relationship. I dipped into my savings and paid for six months' membership.

I didn't meet a long-term partner.

But I did make friends with interesting and genuine people. And I was associating with people who were serious about finding a partner. Even after my membership ended, the Universe continued to bring me opportunities to meet potential partners. One of my new friends recommended a reputable dating website and eight months later I had met the love of my life. He is intelligent, loving, kind, thoughtful, generous of spirit and handsome. We have a wonderful life together.

Expect things to change in a certain way in your life. Hold firmly to that expectation. Move in the direction of that change through even the smallest conscious actions. The Law of Attraction will make change happen. It's inevitable. Know you have the power to rewrite the script of your life. Review the story so far. Take action to make your show reflect the life you want and populate it with great, helpful and stellar cast members.

TRANSFORM YOURSELF, TAKE A SELFIE

Everyone has an idea of how they would like to be regarded. Common to everyone is the desire to feel authentic and whole. The important thing is that there is a match between how you feel on the inside and how you are regarded from the outside. For the majority of us improvements can always be made. Think about what kind of person you really want to be. Think about how you might express that persona. How you present yourself signals, in turn, how you want people to respond to you and the kind of story you want for your future.

You will be surprised how quickly the rest of the world will fall into supporting your authentic self. When you step forward and create the fullest expression of yourself with commitment, your commitment will be mirrored by everyone around you. When a country changes its name to reflect its independent identity, the rest of the international community calls it by its new name and treats it differently. Persia changed its name to Iran. Ceylon changed its name to Sri Lanka. The world didn't say, 'It's not Iran, it's Persia. It's not Sri Lanka, it's Ceylon.' The same is true for individuals. If you say, 'I am this person,' the world will mirror your commitment. It will say, 'Yes you are.' You have only to make a contract with yourself to live authentically and expressively. Children dress up and play different parts in their games with each other all the time. They love taking on different personas and trying them out for size. They're exploring who they are and which expressions of identity suit them best. Why can't this be true for adults? Why is it assumed that adulthood brings with it greater constraints?

Affirm the identity you choose for yourself by taking selfies. Take pictures of yourself when you are feeling most completely like the persona you wish to express. Photograph yourself on the occasions and in the places that best suit your authentic self. Put all these photos in a folder on your phone and look at them often saying to yourself, 'This is who I am. This is the life I am manifesting for myself. I am an adventurer on an adventure of my own choosing.'

Surround yourself with pictures of people and places that reinforce your self-image. If you want to be surrounded by creative people, collect pictures from the internet of artists, designers and writers. If you want to explore spirituality, collect pictures of inspirational speakers and spiritual leaders. Save these pictures on your smart phone and look at them regularly. By picturing yourself in the company of certain types of people, the Universe will bring those people to you. They will be able to guide you further as you express your persona. You will be drawn to things that will support your vision of yourself, a local meditation group or a book club, for example.

The change you want for yourself already exists in the Universe. All you need to do is call it forwards.

Suppose you come across a word that's unfamiliar to you. You look it up in the dictionary to check its meaning and then give it no more thought. Later, you're reading a magazine and there's that word. You're watching the television and there's that word again. Your awareness has connected you to the word and sensitised you to it. Now you see it whenever it occurs where previously you would have been oblivious. The Law of Attraction works in a similar way. The things we want are already present in the potentiality surrounding us. Focusing our attention on them brings them more clearly and sharply into our awareness. It is only then that we are able to grasp them. It is then that they manifest.

Even though I had been to many private views on the London art scene, I could still feel a little uncertain at times. The voice of my inner zombie would say things like, 'You don't fit in here. You're just plain ordinary.' We're all encouraged to operate within predetermined margins of conventionality. In effect, we are encouraged to turn the volume down on expressing our true selves. What happens if you decide to turn the volume back up? This idea freed something inside me. I asked myself, what would I wear if there were no parameters, if there were no conventions. I decided that this forty-something man from Clerkenwell was going to wear paisley shirts and a couple of silver bindi spots. The more I expressed my authentic self in my outward appearance, the more at home I became with my authentic self on the inside. I was influenced less and less by my inner zombie. My narrative was guided increasingly by my inner adventurer. Within weeks, I was feeling at home at each gallery event.

The majority of people are slaves to their inner zombie. They are too busy thinking about themselves to expend energy undermining someone else. Knowing this frees you to be more adventurous in how you present yourself to the world. Build your own truth. Create your own reality. When you give control of your narrative to your inner adventurer, an abundance of good always flows to you. Everybody has interesting and attractive qualities other people love and want to see more of. Often we overlook our own good qualities. Take half an hour to list the great things about you. Try to be clear and level headed about these positive qualities. List as many as you can. Make it a daily practice to look at this list and acknowledge your own value. The more you become aware of the positive aspects of yourself, the more fully you can express them in the world. They become embedded as your internal and external truth.

Sometimes it can be difficult to maintain a positive self-image. Ask yourself, 'If I wanted to persuade someone to live my life for a week, what good things would I tell that person about myself?' Record your ideas on your smart phone. Listen as often as possible. Hearing those positive descriptions of yourself will inspire you. You'll feel appreciation for the good in your life. The frequency of your thoughts will lift attracting more reasons to feel positive and appreciative.

LEARN TO FORGIVE YOUR INNER ZOMBIE

Your inner zombie has always been part of your life. It will always be with you. Your zombie encourages you to think that life is hard. It encourages you to believe you have no control over events and the best you can hope for is survival in the face of adversity. Listen to your zombie and you will conclude that there is greater potential in life for things to go wrong rather than right. Your zombie has had your lifetime to develop this narrative. It has seized on every horror story, every tale of woe since you were small. Your inner zombie is afraid of life. It wants you to settle for less in the mistaken belief that this is where safety lies. It's true that your inner zombie is a problem for you, it is an eternal pessimist but it isn't intrinsically evil. It believes genuinely in its narrative of limitation and lack. It wants your life to remain static and predictable, however poorly that serves you, because it believes this will protect you from misfortune.

Your inner adventurer encourages you to see life as fun. It encourages you to play. It tells you that you do have control over future circumstances. It encourages you to expect the best for your future. If you listen to your adventurer you will see the tremendous potential available to you. Your adventurer will remind you of every success story and all those moments of happiness that have brought you to where you are now. Your inner adventurer loves life. It wants the best for you. It's not afraid of life. It sees nothing to be afraid of. It sees life as a game to be played. It believes in the benevolence of the Universe.

Embrace the potential of your adventurer but don't resent the existence of your zombie. Resentment is a form of attention. Aim to give your inner zombie as little attention as possible. Just let it rest there. Leave it be.

Give attention to your inner zombie only if it has managed to take temporary control of your narrative. Use your awareness to transfer control back to your inner adventurer. Be playful. Laugh at life. Your inner zombie cannot thrive in a playful atmosphere. Play makes your emotional frequency lighter. Play energises your inner adventurer to take back control.

Your inner zombie and your inner adventurer are your lifelong companions. This is a fact of life that you cannot change. But you do have the power to choose which one of them you listen to. We have explored many of the conscious steps you can take to amplify the voice of your inner adventurer. Only that playful inner adventurer can help you manifest the potential and the meaning you want in your life.

PART THREE: KEY IDEAS
Connect with your inner adventurer

i.   Never criticise yourself. Everyone is vulnerable to a zombie attack from time to time. Just take it as a learning opportunity. Be aware. Take action. Redouble your efforts to put your inner adventurer back in control of the story.

ii. Regular check-ins with your abundance buddy help you keep on track. Set regular times to talk in person, by phone, FaceTime, Skype or email.

iii. Compliments are a gift. It is unwise to refuse a compliment because you are effectively denying that quality in yourself. Learn to give and receive compliments graciously and they will increase the sum total of positive energy in your life.

iv. When people speak positively about you, record their comments on your phone.

Look at those comments regularly. This will improve your self-image and your mood. You will attract better experiences to you during the course of your day.

v. Whenever you make a decision ask what stands behind your choice. Is it driven by fear and the expectation of failure or is it driven by a belief in richness of opportunity? If the choice is driven primarily by fear, think again.

vi. When meeting new people, the majority of us mark ourselves down in comparison. When someone is an unknown quantity we tend to assume they are superior. Once you realise this, you can restore the balance. You can choose to mark yourself up and engage with the world on a more equal footing.

vii. Regard everyone you meet as a teacher with a gift to impart, and that is what they will become for you.

viii. We are the authors of our own lives. We write the script of our day-to-day experiences through our thoughts and actions. If you don't like an aspect of the plot you have the power to rewrite it.

ix. Write down the changes you want to make in your storyline. Stick these new plot points on the wall in front of your bed. They will be the first thing you see in the morning and the last thing you see at night. This repeated exposure to your new plot points will help you manifest them powerfully in your future.

x. Create a wall of images of the people you want to see more of. Focus your thoughts on your enthusiasm for these people. The Law of Attraction will bring these people into your life more often.

xi. If you want to live or work in a certain place, spend what time you can there. Play the part of someone who is at home there, rather than merely visiting. Do this with conviction and the Law of Attraction will create the conditions necessary for you to live or work there.

xii. Expect things to change in a certain way in your life. Hold firmly to this expectation. At the same time move towards that change, even in the smallest ways. The Law of Attraction will be mobilised by the firmness of your conviction and the clarity of your action. It will bring you what you focus on.

xiii. How you present yourself to the world signals the person you are and the kind of life you want to live. Express your authentic self boldly and the world will not contradict you, it will follow your lead.

xiv. The Universe never argues. If you say, 'I have a great life. This is who I am. This is the life I am making for myself.' The Universe will respond affirmatively.

xv. Affirm the identity you choose for yourself by taking selfies. Put these in a folder on your phone and look at them often asserting to yourself, 'I am an adventurer on an adventure of my own choosing.'

xvi. Collect pictures from the internet of the kinds of people you want to get to know or the places you want to frequent. Keep them in a file on your phone and look at them often. This regular practice will send a clear message to the Universe so that it can bring these kinds of people and places to you.

xvii. Ask yourself, 'If I wanted to persuade someone to live my life for a week, what good things would I tell that person about myself?' Record your responses on your phone. Play it back to yourself on your way to work, waiting for a friend, whenever you have a few moments. The more you listen, the more you become aware of the good in your life and the more rewarding your life will become.

THE FINAL WORD

THE FINAL WORD

A summary of key ideas from The Zombie Inside

i. The Law of Attraction is a natural law like the law of gravity and, as such, it is acting in all our lives, all of the time.

ii. Bringing positive change into your life through the Law of Attraction is not a quick fix. Some changes can take hours, others days, weeks, months or years. Keep focused and know that the change you want will come.

iii. Everyone is a teacher. Everyone can impart gifts to you about living a better life, just as you can be a great teacher for others. Even challenging people are teaching you something worthwhile. Always ask of every person and situation, 'What is the gift here?'

iv.   Uplifting music to start your day can put you on a positive plane and attract positive experiences throughout your day.

v.   Your abundance buddy can help you work more consistently with the principles of the Law of Attraction. You can share good ideas, positive experiences and ways forward. Have you found your buddy and booked your first check-in?

vi.   Your inner zombie will try to hold you back with limiting beliefs and fear-filled ideas. Through self-observation, you can become aware when this is happening. This awareness is the first critical step to taking back control from your inner zombie.

vii.   When people give you compliments note them down in your phone under the heading 'How others see me'. Whenever your inner zombie tells you that you are not good enough, you'll have hard evidence to the contrary.

viii. Uplifting statements saved as wallpapers on your smart phone can give you a positive thinking boost. Look at your positive wallpaper frequently. The more you focus on it, the more the statement can become true for you.

ix. When people start talking about how bad life is, don't join in unless you want this to become your reality too. Just say to yourself, 'Raise shields! That is not the truth.' Or choose another phrase that works for you to neutralise the negativity of others.

x. Base your decisions on a firm belief that there is richness of opportunity available for all. Be aware that any decision based on fear and limitation is unreliable. Make a vow to be vigilant.

xi. The majority of us have a tendency to mark ourselves down when we meet new people. Restore the balance and mark yourself up.

Respect others but never at the expense of having a healthy respect for yourself.

xii. If someone makes a mistake that affects you negatively, you can choose to take it personally and get caught up in emotional turbulence. Or you can choose to forgive. By choosing forgiveness, you send a message to the Universe that you want to live in a world where forgiveness is the norm.

xiii. You can't change another person. Your only power lies in changing the way you regard and react to that person. Choose to appreciate and focus on the positive aspects of your relationship. What you actively look for, you will see more of.

xiv. It can feel exciting to be 'in on the gossip'. But gossip is always dangerous. Approach life instead like a skilful lawyer making judgments about other people's actions based only on hard evidence.

xv.   You are the scriptwriter of the TV show of your life. Right now you are writing the storyline for future episodes. Check the storyline supports your aims for the future.

xvi.   Write down statements describing any changes to the storyline you want to make. Focus on these new plot points.

xvii.   Develop your friendships consciously. Place pictures on your bathroom mirror of the people you want to see more of. Add the words 'More Please, Thank You' and the Universe will respond accordingly.

xviii. It is not enough to change your thoughts alone. You must also take action, however small, in the direction of the goal you want to achieve.

xix.   If you act with conviction 'as if' something is true, the Universe will take it at face value and make it true.

xx. This work is not about positive thinking in the sense of soldiering on in the face of adversity. It's about positive knowing in the sense of a firm but relaxed expectation that brings about change for the good.

xxi. What are the great qualities about you? Make a list of all your best attributes. Look at them daily.

xxii. Ask yourself, 'If someone were going to live my life for a week, what good things about my life would I tell that person to persuade them to do it?'

xxiii. When you play and have fun in life you release a special kind of energy. You reduce feelings of fear and doubt. You become less emotionally attached to any one outcome. You relax. Ask yourself, 'How can I approach any situation in life in a playful way?'

MOON LARAMIE

Moon Laramie is a spiritual explorer, columnist and meditation teacher. He has been developing his own approaches to spirituality since 2009.

He has encouraged individuals to see the limitless potential available to them through their application of the principles of the Law of Attraction.

As an education adviser he has specialised in strategies to promote well-being. During his time as an adviser for The United Nations Children's Fund he has worked on programmes to raise young people's self esteem and aspirations through equitable rights based approaches to daily living.

The impact of this work has been to empower young people to gain a greater sense of self-worth through an understanding of the interconnectedness they share with others.

With *The Zombie Inside* Moon Laramie brings the distillation and practical application of this knowledge and experience to a new audience of readers and seekers.

Moon Laramie lives and works in Soho, London, England.

www.moonlaramie.com

17066466R00082

Printed in Great Britain
by Amazon